Physical Science
Energy

JACOB BATCHELOR

Children's Press®
An Imprint of Scholastic Inc.

Content Consultant
Valarie Akerson, PhD, Professor of Science Education
Department of Curriculum and Instruction
Indiana University Bloomington, Bloomington, Indiana

Library of Congress Cataloging-in-Publication Data
Names: Batchelor, Jacob, author.
Title: Energy / by Jacob Batchelor.
Description: New York, NY : Scholastic Inc., 2019. | Series: A true book | Includes bibliographical
    references and index.
Identifiers: LCCN 2018034483| ISBN 9780531131381 (library binding) | ISBN 9780531136010 (pbk.)
Subjects: LCSH: Force and energy—Juvenile literature.
Classification: LCC QC73.4 .B39 2019 | DDC 530—dc23
LC record available at https://lccn.loc.gov/2018034483

All rights reserved. Published in 2019 by Children's Press, an imprint of Scholastic Inc.
Printed in North Mankota, MN, USA 113

SCHOLASTIC, CHILDREN'S PRESS, A TRUE BOOK™, and associated logos are trademarks and/or
registered trademarks of Scholastic Inc.

Scholastic Inc., 557 Broadway, New York, NY 10012

1 2 3 4 5 6 7 8 9 10 R 28 27 26 25 24 23 22 21 20 19

**Front cover: Eyjafjallajökull
volcano in Iceland erupting.**

**Back cover: A person seen from between
the Devil's Marbles in Australia**

Find the Truth!

Everything you are about to read is true *except* for one of the sentences on this page.

Which one is **TRUE**?

T or F The sun is fueled by the energy released when atoms inside it break apart.

T or F Plants are humans' main source of chemical energy.

Find the answers in this book.

Contents

THE BIG TRUTH!

Alternative Energy

A student shouting

4

Bonfire

4 Energy and Us

How do we use energy in our daily lives? **33**

Lightbulb

Think About It!

Look closely at the photo on these pages. What do you notice about the image? What do you think is going on? Once you have some predictions about *what* is happening, think about *how* it is happening. What might cause what you see in the photo to occur? What evidence in the photo supports your explanation?

Stumped?
Want to know more? Turn the page!

If you guessed that the photo shows a volcano erupting, you are right! Sakurajima volcano, on page 6, is an active volcano in Kyushu, Japan. Eruptions like that occur when pressure builds deep underground. When that pressure becomes great enough, the top of the volcano explodes. The glowing red lines at the bottom of the photo are streams of molten lava. The large, black cloud contains tiny particles of ash and gases.

Lava shoots from the ground at Hawaii Volcanoes National Park.

Lightning is an example of electricity in nature.

Sometimes, these particles of ash rub together and create an electric charge. If that charge becomes strong enough, lightning forms! This phenomenon is called a dirty thunderstorm.

You might be wondering why a volcanic eruption is in a book about energy. That's because an eruption displays almost all the forms of energy you'll learn about in this book. You'll find that energy is everywhere.

This machine accelerates, or speeds up, particles to 99.99 percent the speed of light!

The Large Hadron Collider uses massive beams of energy to study the universe's smallest particles.

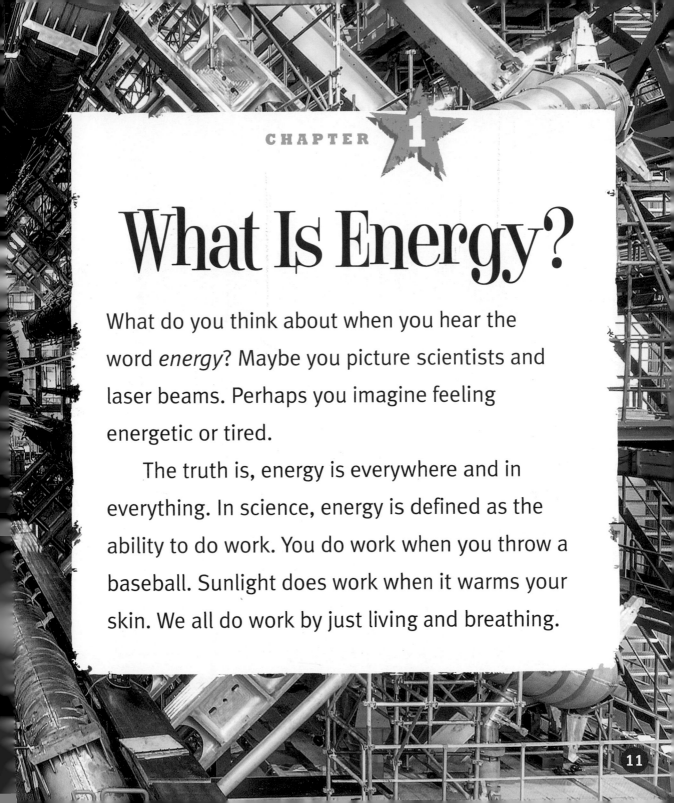

CHAPTER 1

What Is Energy?

What do you think about when you hear the word *energy*? Maybe you picture scientists and laser beams. Perhaps you imagine feeling energetic or tired.

The truth is, energy is everywhere and in everything. In science, energy is defined as the ability to do work. You do work when you throw a baseball. Sunlight does work when it warms your skin. We all do work by just living and breathing.

These boulders have potential energy because they are in a position to fall, and falling is an expression of energy.

Energy at Rest

Energy takes many forms, but most forms are either **potential energy** or **kinetic energy**. Potential energy is energy that is stored, or has the *potential* to do work.

Picture a boulder balanced at the top of a cliff. It's not moving now. But it is full of potential energy. If someone gave it a good push, it would tumble all the way down the cliff. When it hit the bottom, that energy would transfer into the ground.

Energy on the Move

Kinetic energy is energy in motion. Everything that is moving has it. The faster an object moves, the more kinetic energy it has.

Energy can switch between potential and kinetic forms. Kinetic energy can also pass from one object to another. Think about the boulder again. You have kinetic energy when you run toward it. When you push the boulder, you transfer your kinetic energy into it. As the boulder tumbles, its potential energy becomes kinetic energy.

When you run, you have kinetic energy!

The elements inside you are the same elements that make up stars. You are made of stardust!

14

CHAPTER 2

Stored Energy

Potential energy is everywhere because everything—even you—is made up of tiny powerhouses called atoms. Atoms are the smallest unit of an element. There are 7 octillion atoms in every human. That's a 7 followed by 27 zeros! These atoms are held together by superstrong forces. Stored inside each and every atom is a tremendous amount of energy.

Earth's gravity pulls you toward the planet's center.

Gravitational Energy

Imagine yourself on a bike at the top of a big hill. Move forward, and you'll roll all the way down without moving a muscle. How? At the top of the hill, you and your bike are full of energy from gravity, called gravitational energy. Gravity is a force that pulls objects together. Your gravitational energy becomes kinetic energy as you roll downhill. Another example of gravitational energy is the movement of the boulders described on page 12.

Grounded by Gravity

When Earth's gravity pulls us toward the planet's center, it gives us weight. Planets with more mass, such as Jupiter, have a stronger pull. Smaller planets, such as Mars, have a weaker one. You could jump about three times as high on Mars as you can on Earth!

The chart below shows what someone who weighs 100 pounds (45 kilograms) on Earth would weigh on other planetary bodies in the solar system.

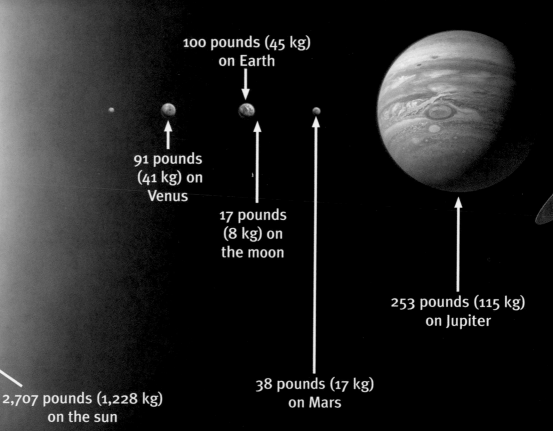

100 pounds (45 kg) on Earth

91 pounds (41 kg) on Venus

17 pounds (8 kg) on the moon

253 pounds (115 kg) on Jupiter

2,707 pounds (1,228 kg) on the sun

38 pounds (17 kg) on Mars

Nuclear Energy

At the center of an atom is its **nucleus**. Tiny particles called protons and neutrons make up the nucleus. Protons have a positive charge. Neutrons have a neutral charge. Smaller particles called electrons circle the nucleus. They have a negative charge.

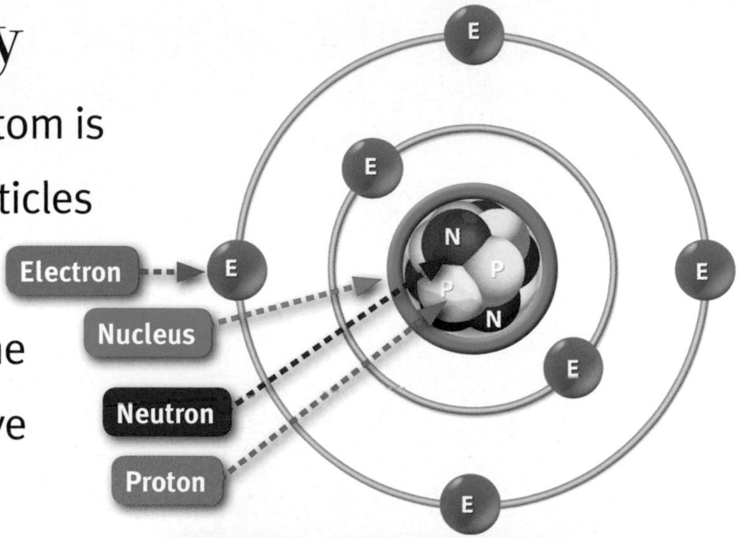

Electron

Nucleus

Neutron

Proton

In the diagram of a carbon atom above, electrons are blue, neutrons are red, and protons are yellow.

The positive force from a proton's charge attracts the negative force from an electron's charge. This attraction holds atoms together. Breaking the bond releases a tremendous amount of energy, called nuclear energy. Nuclear power plants turn this energy into electricity.

Chemical Energy

Chemical energy is essential in day-to-day life. This energy is stored in the bond between molecules. Molecules are made up of two or more atoms joined together. When these bonds break, the energy is released.

All food stores chemical energy. Your stomach breaks down food molecules to release the energy your body needs to function. Batteries also store chemical energy. When they are placed in a phone, watch, or other device, they release the energy.

All the food you eat contains chemical energy.

Plant Power

Plants may not seem very energetic. But they are the source of nearly all the chemical energy humans use every day. Plants use energy from the sun to make food from water, minerals in the soil, and carbon dioxide, a gas present in the atmosphere. Plants store this food in their tissues and leaves. This process is called **photosynthesis**. Humans and other animals eat plants to get energy.

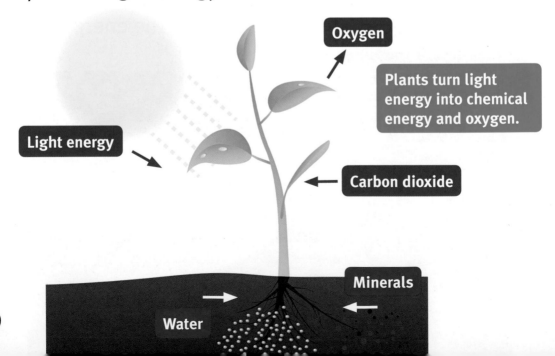

Oxygen

Plants turn light energy into chemical energy and oxygen.

Light energy

Carbon dioxide

Minerals

Water

Burning fossil fuels produces pollution that can harm people and the environment.

Fossil Fuels

Millions of years ago, vast oceans of tiny living things stored chemical energy by soaking up sunlight. Eventually, these living things sank to the ocean floor and became buried. Over the years, heat and pressure turned the living things into oil and natural gas. A similar process formed coal from dead plants in ancient swamps. Humans burn these **fossil fuels** to release their chemical energy. We use that energy for everything from heating homes to driving cars.

A mass of the sun's material, full of energy, erupts from its surface.

Sometimes the sun releases explosions of energy that can travel hundreds of miles per second.

CHAPTER 3

Moving Energy

Kinetic energy is always on the move. But you can't always see it. Some of the most common forms of energy are actually invisible! If you're reading this during the day, just look outside. The sun is the most abundant source of kinetic energy on our planet. Light from the sun allows us to see. It heats our planet. It also provides our plants with energy. Without it, life wouldn't be possible on Earth.

Radiant Energy

Light is a type of radiant energy. It travels in waves. To read this book, your eyes pick up the light waves reflecting off the page or screen. Radiant energy changes depending on how much energy its waves have. This is measured in **wavelengths**. A wavelength is the distance from one wave to the next. Shorter wavelengths have more energy. They are narrow and fast. Longer wavelengths have less energy. They are wider and move more slowly.

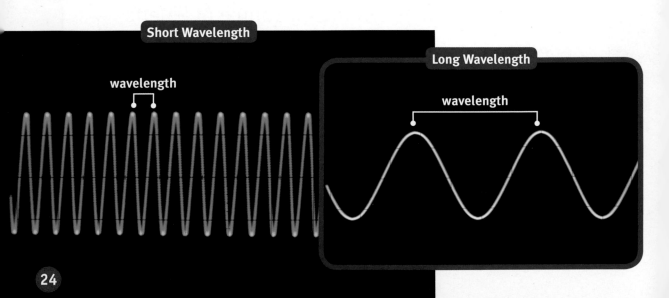

Short Wavelength

wavelength

Long Wavelength

wavelength

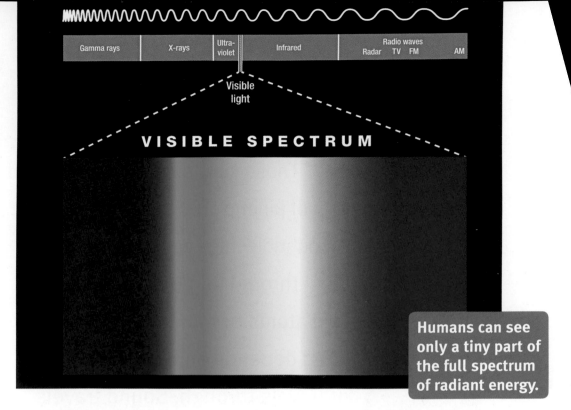

| Gamma rays | X-rays | Ultra-violet | Infrared | Radio waves Radar TV FM | AM |

Visible light

VISIBLE SPECTRUM

Humans can see only a tiny part of the full spectrum of radiant energy.

Would it surprise you to learn that radiant energy is used in radios? What about X-ray machines? There's much more to this energy than what our eyes can see. The electromagnetic **spectrum** contains all these different forms. Radio waves have very long wavelengths and are at one end of the spectrum. X-rays, used for example in medical imaging, have very short wavelengths and are near the other end of the spectrum.

Sound

Open your mouth wide and say "ahhh." Can you feel your throat vibrating? Those vibrations produce sound waves, another form of kinetic energy. Sound waves vibrate tiny atoms and molecules as they travel.

Sound can travel through almost anything, as long as there are atoms or molecules. But its

speed depends on what substance it travels through. Sound travels through the tightly packed atoms of solid objects the fastest. It moves through the more loosely packed atoms of liquids more slowly. It moves slowest through the air, where atoms are far apart.

In general, sound travels more slowly than light.

Tight turns and sudden starts and stops can create friction between a car's tires and the road, producing a lot of heat.

Heat

Here is a quieter trick to try. Rub your hands together as fast as you can. Do you feel the heat? Heat, or thermal energy, is produced by the movement of molecules. The faster molecules move, the more thermal energy they produce. The **friction** from molecules in your hands rubbing together creates the heat you're feeling. Heat is another type of kinetic energy. Don't rub too long or too fast—it might begin to hurt!

Static electricity is one way you experience electricity in nature. Flip to page 40 for an activity to learn more!

Electricity

Electrical energy does more than turn on lightbulbs. It's all around us. It comes from the movement of electrons. Atoms are balanced when they have equal numbers of protons and electrons. But forces, such as rubbing two materials together, can cause atoms to lose electrons. This can lead to the materials being attracted together and a **discharge** as electrons move between atoms to balance positive and negative charges. You've probably experienced this firsthand if you've ever shocked yourself on metal or seen lightning strike.

Flash to BOOM

Lightning strikes produce bright flashes and loud booms. But did you ever notice that you see the lightning before you hear the thunder? Light travels faster than sound does. In fact, you can find your distance from a lightning strike by counting and simple math. When you see a lightning flash, count the seconds it takes to hear a boom. Then divide that number by 5. The result is your approximate distance in miles from the storm!

HOW FAST?	
ENERGY	SPEED
Light from lightning	186,282 miles (299,792 km) per second
Sound from thunder	0.2 miles (0.3 km) per second

Alternative Energy

We use different kinds of energy to power the world around us. The type of energy most widely used comes from burning fossil fuels (coal, oil, and natural gas). This comes at a cost. When burned for energy, fossil fuels give off pollution. Also, supplies are limited.

Luckily, there's an infinite supply of cleaner, alternative energy sources. We can use renewable energy from wind, water, Earth's heat, and the sun to power our lives. These sources produce much less pollution.

Wind farms harness energy from the wind to produce electricity without polluting the air.

Hydroelectric plants turn the power of flowing water into electricity.

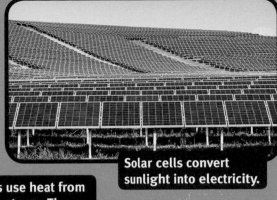

Geothermal plants use heat from the earth to create steam. The steam turns large fans called turbines that create electricity.

Solar cells convert sunlight into electricity.

Types of Energy Used to Produce Electricity in the United States in 2017

Only 15.5 percent of the electricity produced in 2017 came from renewable sources such as geothermal, solar, wind, and hydropower. Fortunately, this number increases every year.

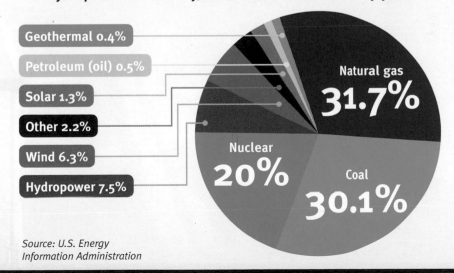

Geothermal 0.4%

Petroleum (oil) 0.5%

Solar 1.3%

Other 2.2%

Wind 6.3%

Hydropower 7.5%

Natural gas 31.7%

Nuclear 20%

Coal 30.1%

Source: U.S. Energy Information Administration

Fire produces two types of energy: light and heat.

CHAPTER 4

Energy and Us

Life needs energy. Early humans burned wood for heat and to cook food. Modern life, from lightbulbs to smartphones, would be impossible if we hadn't learned how to use all the different types of energy around us.

Powering the Planet

Today, we generate electricity at power plants.
Most power plants use an energy source to heat
water into steam. The steam turns turbines, or
large fans. These turbines generate electricity as
they spin. The electricity flows through wires that
carry it to homes, businesses, and other buildings.

Timeline of Energy Through the Ages

1,000,000–200,000 BCE
Humans learn to create and control fire.

644 CE
The first known working windmill is built in present-day Iran.

1,000,000–200,000 BCE → 200 BCE → 644 CE → 1859

About 200 BCE
People in China begin working in the world's first recorded coal mine.

1859
Workers in Pennsylvania drill the first oil well in the United States.

Almost all power plants work this way. Coal-fired power plants burn coal to produce heat. Natural gas power plants burn gas. Even alternative energy plants use the same basic process. Geothermal plants use heat energy from deep within Earth to heat water and create steam. Solar thermal plants use heat energy from the sun to drive their turbines. At hydroelectric plants, water turns the turbines.

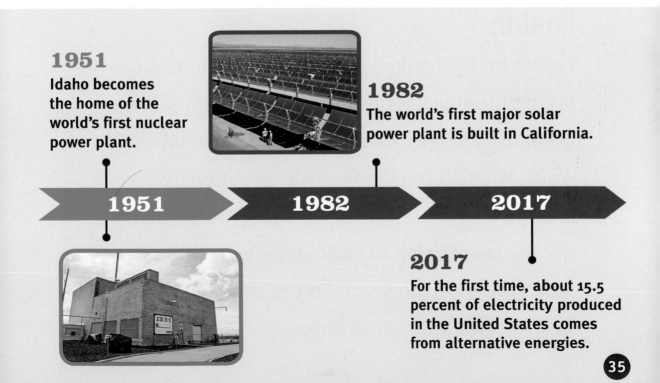

1951
Idaho becomes the home of the world's first nuclear power plant.

1982
The world's first major solar power plant is built in California.

1951   1982   2017

2017
For the first time, about 15.5 percent of electricity produced in the United States comes from alternative energies.

Fusion

Earlier in this book, you learned that there is a lot of potential energy stored inside atoms. This potential energy can be released in two different ways. You can see the first way in action just by looking at the sun. The sun's energy is fueled by the **nuclear fusion** of hydrogen deep within its fiery core. This process involves combining—or fusing—two atoms into one.

Fission

Closer to home, the second type of nuclear energy powers many people's daily lives. **Nuclear fission** is the splitting of an atom's nucleus to release heat energy. In nuclear power plants, this process produces tremendous amounts of heat. This heat creates steam that powers turbines. Fission is also the process that makes atomic bombs so dangerous. These weapons split atoms to release earth-shattering amounts of energy.

In most nuclear power plants, steam from super-heated water escapes through giant chimneys.

Future of Energy

Now that you understand the basics of energy, you can dream about where this knowledge might take you. All around the world, scientists and engineers are using these same basic concepts to solve big problems. Would you like to create the next generation of clean, alternative energy? Do you want to research the mysteries of the cosmos? You can change the world tomorrow by using the knowledge you're learning today. Good luck!

People are constantly researching new ways to create, control, and use energy.

The Future of Energy Is You!

Would you like to work in science? Here are just a few of the exciting careers that focus on the many aspects of energy.

- **Sound engineers** study sound waves to help make concerts sound amazing.

- **Particle physicists** use huge machines to study the tiniest building blocks of the universe.

- **Wind engineers** climb massive wind turbines to tinker with powerful engines.

- **Nuclear physicists** keep nuclear power plants running safely and smoothly.

- **Electricians** study and control the flow of electricity through circuits.

- **Space engineers** determine the energy needed for rockets to escape Earth's gravity and function in space. ★

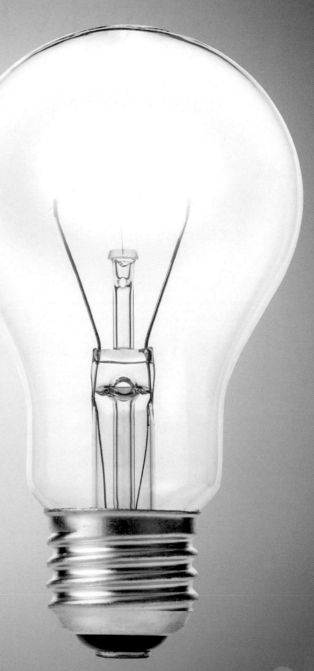

Sticky Balloon!

In this investigation, you will learn more about static electricity, or the buildup of charges on an object.

Materials

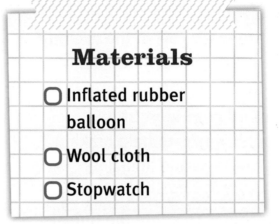

- ☐ Inflated rubber balloon
- ☐ Wool cloth
- ☐ Stopwatch

Directions

1. Set your balloon and cloth in front of you. At rest, your balloon and cloth have a neutral, or no, charge.

2. Hold the balloon against a wall. Start the stopwatch and let go of the balloon. How long does it take the balloon to reach the floor?

3. Rub the balloon with the cloth for 10 seconds. This builds up a negative charge. Then repeat step 2. The balloon's negative charge is attracted to the wall, which is more positively charged. Does this change how long the balloon stays up?

4. Repeat step 3 several times, adding 10 more seconds of rubbing each time. Does the balloon take a longer or shorter time to reach the ground the more you rub?

Explain It!

Using what you learned in this book, can you explain why the balloon stays up longer the longer you rub it with the cloth? If you need help, turn back to page 28 for more information.

Sensing Sound!

In this investigation, you will learn more about how sound waves travel.

Materials

- ☐ 4-foot piece of yarn
- ☐ Metal spoon
- ☐ Ruler

Directions

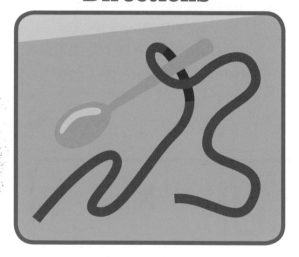

1. Tie the yarn around the spoon with the spoon at the center of the yarn. Pull both ends of the yarn so the loop tightens around the handle.

2. Hold each end of the yarn against the openings of your ears. The spoon should hang at about the height of your waist.

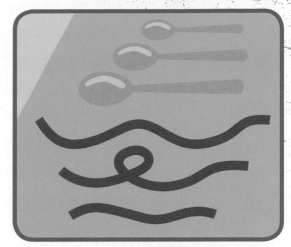

3. Have a friend gently tap the spoon with the ruler. What do you hear? What does your friend hear?

4. Try changing the length of the yarn or using a different-sized spoon. What changes do you notice? Trade places with your friend. What changes do you notice?

Explain It!

Using what you learned in this book, can you explain how the sound travels along the string? How does it change when the string is longer? If you need help, turn back to page 26 for more information.

True Statistics

The speed of light: 186,282 mi. per second (299,792 km per second)

The speed at which sound travels through air: 1,087 ft. per second (331 m per second)

The speed at which sound travels through water: 4,921 ft. per second (1,500 m per second)

Percentage of U.S. electricity produced by renewable energy sources in 2017: 15.5

Percentage of U.S. electricity produced by nuclear power in 2017: 20

Percentage of U.S. electricity produced by fossil fuels in 2017: 62.3

Amount of electricity generated by a lightning strike: 1 billion volts

Did you find the truth?

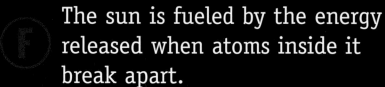

F The sun is fueled by the energy released when atoms inside it break apart.

T Plants are humans' main source of chemical energy.

44

Resources

Books

Bang, Molly. *Buried Sunlight: How Fossil Fuels Have Changed the Earth.* New York: Blue Sky/Scholastic, 2014.

Green, Dan. *Eyewitness: Energy.* New York: DK Publishing, 2016.

Ives, Rob. *Fun Experiments with Electricity: Mini Robots, Micro Lightning Strikes, and More.* Minneapolis: Lerner Publications, 2018.

Kenney, Karen Latchana. *Energy Investigations.* Minneapolis: Lerner Publishing Group, 2018.

Visit this Scholastic website for more information on Energy:
 www.factsfornow.scholastic.com
Enter the keyword **Energy**

Important Words

discharge (DIS-chahrj) to release into the open

fossil fuels (FAH-suhl FYOOLZ) fuels such as coal, oil, and natural gas that are formed from the remains of prehistoric plants and animals

friction (FRIK-shuhn) the force that slows down objects when they rub against each other

kinetic energy (kih-NET-ik EN-ur-jee) energy that is in motion

nuclear fission (NOO-klee-ur FISH-uhn) energy created by splitting the nucleus of an atom

nuclear fusion (NOO-klee-ur FYOO-zhun) energy created by combining the nuclei of two atoms

nucleus (NOO-klee-us) the central part of an atom that is made up of neutrons and protons

photosynthesis (foh-toh-SIN-thih-sis) a chemical process in which green plants and other organisms use the sun's energy to turn water and carbon dioxide into food

potential energy (puh-TEN-shuhl EN-ur-jee) energy that is stored

spectrum (SPEK-truhm) a sequence or range, such as the light spectrum

wavelengths (WAYV-lengkths) distances between a point on one wave of light or sound and the same point on the next

Index

Page numbers in **bold** indicate illustrations.

About the Author

Jacob Batchelor studied English and creative writing at Dartmouth College in New Hampshire, and he currently writes and edits science-focused stories for Scholastic's *Science World*. When he's not hanging out in the library or writing books for kids, he likes to take long walks in Prospect Park near his home in Brooklyn, New York.